© 1989 Franklin Watts

Franklin Watts
12a Golden Square
London W1R 4BA

Franklin Watts Australia
14 Mars Road
Lane Cove
N.S.W. 2066

ISBN: 0 86313 820 9

Design: Edward Kinsey
Typesetting: Lineage, Watford
Printed in Italy
by G. Canale & C.S.p.A, Turin

The publishers, author and photographer would like to thank Bob Stock, Alan Payne and Nigel Andrews of Unigate Dairies for their help and co-operation in the preparation of this book.

Milkman

Tim Wood
Photographs: Chris Fairclough

Franklin Watts
London · New York · Sydney · Toronto

I am a milkman.

I deliver milk.

When I arrive at the depot,
I unplug the electric charger
from my milk float.

I collect crates of milk from the cold store.

I load the crates of milk on to my milk float.

I collect other food and drinks from a special locker which I filled yesterday.

I load the food
into a large cold box
on the back of my milk float.

A checker makes a note of everything I have taken.

I leave the depot
and start my delivery round.

I deliver
my first bottles of milk
before most people are awake.

I leave
the correct amount of milk
and take away the empty bottles.

I deliver most milk to the door, but sometimes I leave it at the gate!

I carry
several different types of milk,
soft drinks and foods.

Some people leave the money for the milk on the doorstep.
I must count it carefully.

Sometimes people buy
milk or food
straight from the milk float.

Once a week I collect money for the milk I have delivered.

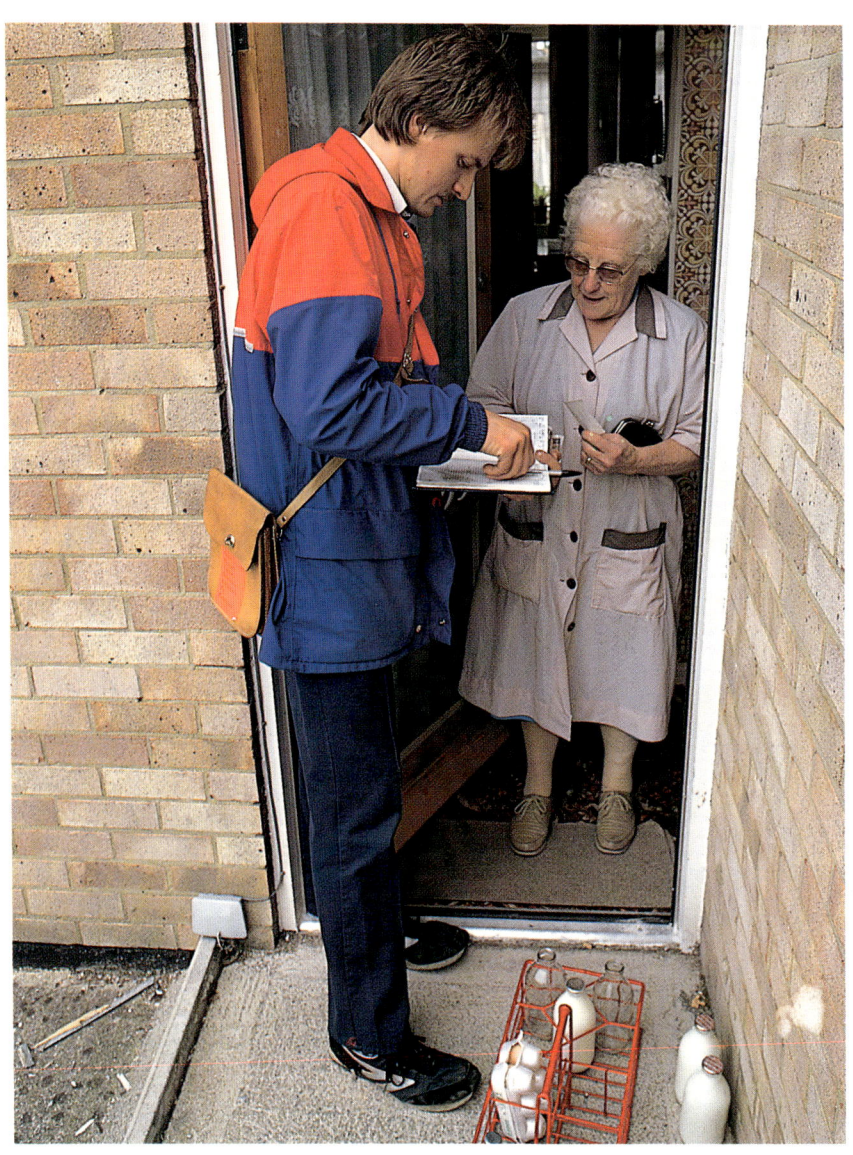

I sell other food while I collect the milk money.

I write down everything I sell and all the money I collect in a special book.

When my round is finished,
I return my unsold milk
to a special cold store.

In the office I count out the money I have collected and hand it in.

FACTS ABOUT MILKMEN

The milkman writes in his book how much milk and other goods his customers want each day. He also writes exactly where they want him to leave it. If the milkman goes on holiday, the relief milkman knows by reading the book how much milk to leave and where it should be put.

A milkman works from about 4 o'clock in the morning until mid-day. On collection days the round may not finish until 2 o'clock in the afternoon.

Milkmen spend over five weeks learning how to do their job. They spend two weeks with an experienced milkman called a supervisor. Then they go to a training school for milkmen where they learn about the milk industry, how to fill in their book and how to add up the money they collect. They then spend three weeks going round with another milkman, learning about the round they will be doing.

The milkman always takes extra milk and food in case anyone wants more than usual.

GLOSSARY

Cold box
A large refrigerator (fridge) on the back of the milk float for storing food. It is powered by batteries under the milk float.

Cold store
A building which is a huge refrigerator (fridge). It is used for storing the milk to keep it cool and fresh.

Depot
The milkman's base. It is a group of buildings which include the offices, the stores and the garages for the milk floats.

Electric charger
Electric cables which pass electricity into the milk float's batteries.

Locker
A cage which can be locked. In it the milkman stores overnight the food he will take with him the next day. The lockers are in a cold store to keep the food fresh.

Relief milkman
A milkman who stands in for another milkman who is ill or on holiday.

Round
The route followed by the milkman each day.

INDEX

Batteries 28
Book 23, 27
Bottle 15, 16, 24, 25, 28

Checker 13, 28
Crates 9, 10, 28
Cold box 12, 28
Cold store 9, 24, 27, 28
Collection day 27, 28
Customers 27

Delivery round 14
Depot 8, 14, 28

Electric charger 8, 28

Food 11, 12, 18, 20, 22, 28

Locker 11, 28

Milk 7, 9, 10, 15, 16, 17, 18, 19, 20, 21, 24, 27, 28
Milkman 7, 27, 28
Milk float 8, 10, 12, 20, 28

Money 19, 21, 22, 23, 26, 27, 28

Relief milkman 27, 28
Refrigerator 27, 28
Round 14, 24, 27, 28

Soft drinks 18